Huffkin

Written by Pip Jones

Illustrated by Alice Wong

Collins

Gran's garden had a swing and green trees with pink flowers. The best thing for Gus was ... Huffkin!

Snort!

3

Gran said, "Huffkin is my sweet animal pal. I see her in my garden at night."

5

Gran added three spoonfuls of cat food
to a dish.

7

That night, Huffkin was
chomping and snorting in
Gran's garden.

Gus kept back and didn't approach.
He greeted Huffkin with a grin.

Then one morning, Gran said,
"It's winter, so Huffkin must sleep
until spring."

Gran put Huffkin's nest between the shed and tree. They spotted Huffkin creeping there in the moonlight.

All winter, Gus was helpful to Gran by painting, clearing up and sweeping.
It was fun!

In March, the pink flowers were back.
And so was ...

Huffkin!

Snort!

13

In Gran's garden

After reading

Letters and Sounds: Phase 4

Word count: 154

Focus on adjacent consonants with long vowel phonemes, e.g. /g/ /r/ /ee/ /n/

Common exception words: of, to, the, all, by, put, my, he, she, we, was, they, said, so, were, there, one

Curriculum links: Science: Animals, including humans

National Curriculum learning objectives: Spoken language: listen and respond appropriately to adults and their peers; Reading/word reading: read other words of more than one syllable that contain taught GPCs; Reading/comprehension: understand books they can already read accurately and fluently, draw on what they already know or on background information and vocabulary provided by the teacher; make inferences on the basis of what is being said and done

Developing fluency

- Your child may enjoy hearing you read the book.
- Turn to page 5. Model reading the speech appropriately.
- Now ask your child to read the speech bubbles on pages 7 and 13 with expression.

Phonic practice

- Model sounding out the following word, saying each of the sounds quickly and clearly. Then blend the sounds together. Ask your child to do the same.

  g/r/ee/n   **green**

- Point to the beginning two letters in the word **green**. Now look at page 7. Can your child find any other words that begin with these two letters? (*grain*)
- Now ask your child to sound out and blend the following words:

  snort   clear   approach   spoonfuls

Extending vocabulary

- Flick through the book together and look for all the verbs that show what Huffkin does. (*chomping, snorting, creeping*)
- Now ask your child to find the verbs that show what Gus does on page 12. (*painting, clearing, sweeping*)
- Can they think of any other verbs that Huffkin might do? (e.g. *sniffing, rolling, curling, sleeping*)